Prayer and Poetry

by Helen C. White

Wimmer Lecture VIII

THE ARCHABBEY PRESS

Latrobe, Pennsylvania

Distributed by

University Publishers, Inc.
59 East 54th Street
New York 22, N.Y.

Nihil obstat: Francis J. Mueller
Deputatus ad hoc

Imprimatur: ✠Wm. G. Connare
Episcopus Greensburghensis
July 11, 1960—Feast of the
Solemnity of Saint Benedict

Wimmer Lecture VIII

Saint Vincent College
Latrobe, Pennsylvania

The Wimmer Lecture

During the centenary year of Saint Vincent Archabbey and College the Board of Trustees of the College established an annual lecture in honor of the Right Reverend Archabbot Boniface Wimmer, O.S.B. It was on October 18, 1846, that Boniface Wimmer, with his small band of Pioneers, arrived at St. Vincent and began the first permanent Benedictine foundation in North America. From this archabbey numerous other Benedictine abbeys have sprung, directly or indirectly. They carry on the monastic life and conduct schools and colleges in many parts of the United States and Canada.

By a memorial at once fitting and significant the Wimmer Lecture seeks to keep alive and in grateful remembrance the name of this good and great man. Each year on some convenient day, preferably near December 8th, the anniversary of his death, it brings before the members of the institution he founded a distinguished scholar, whose lecture is subsequently printed in the form of a small book. The lecturer is free to choose his own subject.

Following is the list of Wimmer Lecturers with their topics:

Prayer and Poetry

PRAYER AND POETRY, WHILE DIFFER-ing profoundly in their surface mani-festations, have fundamentally very much in common. Both spring from the same deep ground of the spirit which has commanded man's fascinated attention from the dawn of consciousness, and which still eludes his most sophisticated probings in even this most self-conscious of centuries. Those hardy pioneers of the mind, the ancient Greeks, recognized the ageless challenge in the legend they put above the portals of the Oracle at Delphi, "Γνῶθι σεαυτόν," "Know thyself," and in the speculations of their wisest and greatest, Socrates, Plato, Aristotle, discovered that they had embarked on an unending quest.

And conversely, some eight centuries later another hardy adventurer into the undiscovered realms of the spiritual universe found that all searchings came home to that familiar mystery. "O Thou Beauty of ancient days, yet ever new!" cried Saint Augustine of Hippo in one of the most ringing passages of his *Confessions,* "Too late I loved Thee! And behold, Thou wert within, and I abroad, and there I searched for Thee; deformed I, plunging amid those fair forms, which Thou hadst made."[1]

But as both the Greeks and Saint Augustine so well knew, it is no simple thing for man to penetrate into that realm within himself, and it is hardly to be wondered at that he shrinks from attempting it unless he is driven to it by what amounts almost to compulsion. It takes a very special kind of experience to disturb the calm waters of everyday acceptance and shake the consciousness out of its lethargy and its complacency. And this is true both for the poet and the man of prayer, for diverse as the manifestations of poetry and prayer often are —even on occasion to what seem the extremes of opposition—both have their roots in the same type of experience. The first mark of this experience is surprise, with its handmaid, wonder. The great poet-critic of the English Romantic Movement put it very well for the poets when he said it was the part of his friend Wordsworth in the epoch-making *Lyrical Ballads:* ''to give the charm of novelty to things of every day, and to excite a feeling analogous to the supernatural, by awakening the mind's attention from the lethargy of custom, and directing it to the loveliness and the wonders of the world before us."[2] The masters of the spiritual life have, also, agreed that the distinctive mark of high religious experience is that it makes all things new, and particularly the man who beholds them. So the converted Paul exhorts the Romans to "walk in newness of life"[3] and the Ephesians to put on the "new man."[4] Men have long tried to explain what it is that creates this extraordinary disturbance in the depths of the consciousness. Some years ago a German writer, Rudolph Otto, in his analysis of what might be called the concept of the holy, suggested the term, the "numinous."[5]

This sense of something divine is a very general thing, for the experience is a widely diffused one. Sometimes it attaches itself to places. One recalls the Lord's admonition to

Moses in Exodus, "Draw not nigh hither: put off thy shoes from off thy feet, for the place whereon thou standest is holy ground."[6] The Old Testament is full of such episodes, and so is classic literature. More often it is people who give this sense of the presence of the divine. The famous definition of the small boy in a stained-glass window parish, that saints are people through whom the light shines, expresses a very ancient experience. One thinks of the Apostles and their unrecognized Companion on the road to Emmaus—"Did not our heart burn within us, while he talked with us by the way?"[7] And, on the other hand, the lover's sense that there is something divine in the object of his love is not lightly to be dismissed either as blasphemy or hyperbole. This sense of the numinous is the common ground both of poetry and of prayer.

I have said the experience is disturbing and that is true. Divinity is too much for the finite spirit. One hides one's face; one seeks relief from the unexpected burden. There is something of terror in all awe, as Aristotle understood very well,[8] and the mortal spirit seeks refuge from it. And yet there is a magnetism about the numinous. It pulls the sensitive spirit out of the safe refuge of its mediocrity. Like a child, one is afraid, and yet one cannot but draw near. All the world's great religions have recognized in this fascination the evidence of the soul's inalienable participation in the divine. One is both frightened of the divine and yet one aches to possess it. St. Augustine, who so often spoke for all of us with that varicolored experience of his, put it in religious terms: "Thou madest us for Thyself, and our heart is restless, until it repose in Thee."[9]

One may shudder at the lover's deification of his beloved, but I am not sure that there isn't an even greater audacity in the worshipper's laying hold upon the feet of his divinity. That is, perhaps, the secret of the paradox of his behavior. The very experience of the divine carries one out beyond himself, and yet he aches to bring it home. One wishes to surrender all outmoded impulse to action, and yet one wishes to do something about the wonder he has known. The scene on the Mount of the Transfiguration is really a parable for all contact with the divine, both secular and religious, and even if he did not know what he said, Peter expressed a deep human impulse when he suggested that they erect the three tabernacles.[10]

There are, I think, several reasons for this absurdly incommensurate creative impulse. First of all, there is the very human desire for commemoration. The very experience of the numinous is like all intense experience, fleeting. Indeed, the frailty of humanity could not sustain it if it were otherwise. And yet one yearns to preserve at least some shadow of the radiance one has known. It is not simply a matter of remembering what has been seen, or heard, or touched. It is, also, a matter of preserving something even more fleeting, and that is the reaction of the person who saw and heard. And here, I think, we come close to the secret of the power of the numinous— that is, its dynamic quality. For the divine is not only the perfection, which we all recognize, though afar off, as the bourne toward which we are, however unsteadily, moving, but the divine is, also, the life-giving, the life-stirring. It is the very creative dynamic of divinity that makes the experience of the numinous so profoundly disturbing. He who has, however remotely, come into contact with the creative vitality of the divine is moved himself to creation.

This is pre-eminently true of the poet, especially of that type of poet who is closest to the man who prays, and that is the lyric poet, who is primarily concerned with telling directly of his own experience. Our forefathers in the language we speak called the poet a "maker," a man who makes something. He makes something out of the common materials of his craft, in this case out of words, the counters of men's exchange of perception and thought and feeling. Words are symbols, and yet they have, also, their own history of associations and meanings, and their own capacities of suggestion and of evocation, their own possibilities of pattern-making and of music, heard and unheard—in short, their own mysterious dynamic, reaching backward and forward with their ministry to ear and mind. The poet makes something, something elusive and full of power and meaning.

This thing which the poet makes is like everything in man's handling of the numinous, so complicated that paradox only seems competent to deal with it. The poet tries to record the data of his experience, not so much "This is," as "This I have seen," "This I have felt." He wishes, first of all, like everyone who has known the numinous, to preserve it for himself, though even as he strains to grasp it, it recedes like the face of Eurydice through the shadows of the Lower World. He tries also to communicate it. This is still more hazardous, for here he must appeal to a common ground of human experience, and of this one can never be sure. In the beginning one thinks one's experience is unique, and then one discovers how common it is. Only later does one discover how elusive the common can be. Its very familiarity is deceiving, so that recognition can betray, and yet one must appeal to this common ground—knowing how hazardous it is. Even the most limited statement is like the steam whistle of a train, echoing through the night, taking on fresh mystery with each reverberation through the darkness.

It is not only memory that is tricky here, but attention itself. Even a photograph selects in its light and shadow; and the poet, with the basically unmechanical structure of man's mind, selects more rigorously still. However he may struggle to present the thing he has experienced in its purity, it is saturated with his feeling, and there is nothing static about feeling. It evokes fresh feeling, and the veils fall over the object. The ancient world with its passion for clarity and order, with its emphasis on the unmoved steadiness of pure being, used the word "imitation" for the "making" of the poet. We today, triumphant in our conquest of the material world around us and baffled by our confusion before the mystery of the world within, find imitation too limited a concept. We use "symbol." And yet I am not sure that "symbol" is adequate, for this which the poet creates is something highly dynamic. It is, if one may use the word for what is itself so characteristically unmechanical, a sort of mechanism. It is like those ingenious contrivances which transform sound into light. A poem is a new focus of energy, the organization of a new center of action.

Prayer and Poetry

It is not quite a living thing, but it reveals new facets of experience, and it affects our sensibilities like something living, and to the extent of its influence it leads us further into the fullness of life.

I have used the word "mechanism" as a general term for something which impresses and modifies the consciousness of other people, but it is, as we have seen, a highly incalculable business. And yet if there is one point at which the maker of a poem differs from the rest of us, it is in his passion for precision. He wants to get to the heart of his experience, to its essence, just as directly as he can. Most of us go through life on a hit-and-run basis, smearing the fragments of the universe we pass with loose identifications and vaguer reactions. But it is of the essence of the poet that he will spare no pains to get to the heart of his experience and no expense to put it as precisely as he can. The average man says, "I know what I mean even if I can't say it," but the poet shudders at such crass defeatism. He will agonize until he gets as close as he can to what it is he is trying to talk about; and like an oculist adjusting a lens, he will stop only when he finds that he is beginning to blur what he has done. In a sense, therefore, the completion of any poem is for the poet but an armistice in a battle which he can neither win nor give up.

As for him who hears or reads, we should never lose sight of the plain fact that all effort at communication is a casting of bread upon the waters. Once the poem is sung or printed, then the frail craft is quite literally launched upon unknown seas. It may come home to friendly ports, but to full understanding never. Like all the forms of creation the poem has taken on an independent life of its own beyond its maker's control. But even if the poet has failed to do what he set out to do, he has also done something beyond his dreams. What Longinus said of the sublime is true of all the poetic modes: "For in some natural fashion our soul is elevated by the truly sublime, and assuming a lofty stature is filled with delight and proud elation, as if she herself had brought forth what she has merely heard."[11] This is true, above all, of that poetry which undertakes to deal with the more direct and the more specific experience of the divine, what we may call the poetry of prayer.

The distinctive thing about prayer, I need hardly remind you, is that it is addressed directly to God, and that all that it treats of is presented in the context of that Presence. Incidentally, of course, one learns a good deal from a man's prayer of his experience, and even of what kind of person he is. But that is by the way. The invocation of the presence of God is the focussing factor of this particular handling of human experience. It is important, therefore, that prayer should be taken neither thinly nor narrowly. All too many men have read only the first half of the Gospel sentence: "Ask and ye shall receive; seek and ye shall find; knock and it shall be opened unto you."[12] Yearning and fear, of course, have their place, for in yearning is man's greatest ambition, and in fear, when it is not illusion, the profoundest recognition of his limitations. But love should have its way in thanksgiving, and that which endows the poet with all the riches of the universe, the praise of the Creator through His works. Of course, man stands on tiptoe, as it were, in prayer, and yet in the presence of his Maker it would be absurd for him to pretend to be above himself or to deny his own nature.

There are two things, therefore, that prayer needs more than anything else. It needs realism, and it needs courage. That is why it is hard to write a good prayer, and why, too, the world's great prayers affect us like a trumpet call. They stir in us depths of feeling that we did not know we possessed, and they waken in us powers beyond our reach. Saint Augustine came pretty close to putting it in a sentence when he prayed, "Narrow is the mansion of my soul; enlarge Thou it, that Thou mayest enter in."[13] Prayers like this have the power and the dynamic of great poetry. And always they have the extraordinary freshness and relevance of great poetry because they have that same power of bringing alive and making live.

And yet it is much harder than most people

think to write good religious poetry because two standards must be met in the effort. As Mr. T. S. Eliot, who has an eminent right to speak of such matters, has very well put it, "The capacity for writing poetry is rare; the capacity for religious emotion of the first intensity is rare; and it is to be expected that the existence of both capacities in the same individual should be rarer still."[14] The two capacities are not by any means unrelated, but they are very different, and one cannot be substituted for the other.

In some companies I should stress the fact that poetry cannot take the place of prayer. But in this company, where a respect for prayer may be taken for granted, I am going to stress the other side. We have all of us known religious poetry that, like other forms of religious art, relied upon edification for its appeal and claimed our tolerance on the grounds of our common piety. Insignificant as it was from the aesthetic point of view, it yet had a kind of whole-hearted sincerity about it that made even the critic feel diffident. Even though he knew that it was pretty feeble poetry, he recognized uncomfortably that the man who wrote it was a better man than he. Such humility will, of course, do the critic no harm, for the exercise of his profession is hardly conducive to humility. But it is bad for poetry and bad for piety, too. The good intention may and ought to move Christian compassion, but it is not enough to redeem the artistic failure; and when, as so often happens, the mediocrity of expression but thinly veils conventionality of thought and feeling, then like any other form of bad art, it becomes a menace to religion. Divine compassion—happily for all of us—may be counted on not to despise anyone's poor best. But even divine compassion ought not to be imposed upon too often; and from the purely human point of view, the complacency one too often encounters in pious ineptitude comes pretty close to blasphemy. It is no wonder that many people have come to feel that religious verse is at best a dull business.

The fact is that good religious poetry takes the very best of what the poet and religious man has to offer in both capacities, and the magnitude of this dual undertaking is not to be underestimated by either poet or reader. For the man who aspires to write really good religious poetry is from the beginning haunted by the paradox that while he cannot resist the urge to expression, what he has to say is ultimately beyond expression. The contemplative, who goes furthest in the penetration of this area of human experience, might be deemed especially well equipped for this undertaking, particularly when he happens to be a master of words, too. But here some highly articulate men have been reduced to something very much like stammering, and it is not for any want of grasp on what they are trying to put into words. Even Saint Bernard of Clairvaux, who in his great series of sermons on the *Canticle of Canticles* comes perhaps as close as anyone to giving a direct prose account of contemplative experience, confesses himself baffled and takes refuge in the fact of the transforming effect of the presence of the Divine: "It was not by His motions that He was recognized by me, nor could I tell by any of my senses that He had penetrated to the depths of my being. It was . . . only by the revived activity of my heart that I was enabled to recognize His Presence."[15]

The difficulty is a basic one. The poet deals with the things of this world as they come to his senses, and as he reacts to them. His senses are more discriminating, more alert, more responsive to the look and sound and feel and taste of this world about him than are those of the rest of us, but like all of us he is subject to their limitations. Furthermore, the art which he practices is dependent upon the world of the senses for the color and suggestiveness of imagery and the magic of verbal music. The clearer, the sharper, the more immediately moving the image, the better the poem in general, and likewise the more swiftly and surely the music of the verse picks up the pitch of the poet's emotion, the more certainly will it carry us along on the rhythm of his experience. But in the case of the religious lyrist the higher he soars toward the Divine, which is his theme and his objective, the more he is dazzled by the light of the ineffable, of that which by definition is beyond the reach and compass of the senses, and the more he is baffled when he tries to make his report. Indeed, the very effort to make a report is in effect a suspension of a journey, the end of which is silence, and every religious poet is at last, like Mallarmé's Saint, a "Musician of Silence."[16] And yet finding words for what he feels is the calling, the very excuse for being, of the poet. It is not surprising, then, that for this most fresh and unique of experiences he reaches out for help to other men, his predecessors and his contemporaries alike. For both poetry and religion have this in common, that though they involve the most personal and individual of the elements of human experience, they also involve the tradition in which a man lives and works. The simplest thing we think, or feel, or say about God involves not only revelation but centuries of human experience. Even Our Lord used the Old Testament for the human terms in which He gave His message, even in his last cry of desolation from the Cross echoing the Psalmist.[17] And the same is true of the poets. The most original never begins quite all over again. The very language he uses represents centuries of struggle for definition.

And particularly is this true when the poet resorts to symbolism to body forth what he has to say. All Christian poets in varying degrees use the psalms, the great quarry of Christian poetry, the very syllabary of Christian devotion. And, as poets always have, they

use the work of their predecessors for inspiration, and suggestion, and even forthright
borrowing. The debt of Thomas Aquinas in
Lauda Sion to Adam of St. Victor,[18] and in
Pange lingua to the *Pange lingua gloriosi pro-
elium certaminis* of Venantius Fortunatus in the
Corpus Christi office is a good example.[19]
And yet just as many of us Americans in particular need to be reminded that the most
contemporary of poetry involves an ancient
heritage, so, also, we Christians who are ac-
customed to think of tradition and inheritance
whenever we think of the faith need to remind
ourselves that not the least of the miracles of
our faith is that it is perpetually renewed, and
that even the timeless is given fresh example
and fresh realization in the mesh of the contemporary.

Now if that task of making the timeless at

home in the distractions and confusions of the present day seems pretty appalling to face, we might take a look at how some of the great Christian lyrics came into being, say, some of the classics of the missal. We know from Saint Augustine that the great Ambrosian hymns had their origin in the fierce turmoil of the church-state conflicts of the fourth century.[20] Much has been said of the serene Roman objectiveness of these compositions that were to transform the church services of that day and beget so distinguished a progeny in the centuries to come.

But it is hard to imagine anything less serene than the New Basilica of Milan in the year 386, jammed with the supporters of the great Catholic bishop, a large part of the populace of Milan, watching and praying day and night for the success of his resistance to the Arians, with the Gothic troops of the Emperor pressing around the very doors. Ambrose himself was by inheritance and upbringing a far purer and more complete representative of the Roman aristocrat than any of the semi-barbarian emperors of his day. But Roman aristocrat as he was, Ambrose was a sensitive and skilled popular leader. And he saw that enthusiasm needed reinforcement if the instinctive rally of the populace was to be transformed into the kind of resistance that would sustain a siege. So he set himself to the composition of songs that the simplest of his people could sing with understanding and pleasure.[21] And mindful as he always was of the teaching function of the bishop, he took the opportunity which these songs offered of teaching his people, or perhaps more accurately, of strengthening their grip on the basic

Christian truths of which the emperors had so often shown themselves so careless. It was, altogether, a superb device which modern propaganda and public relations experts might envy. And we can imagine the crowd of weary and anxious watchers brightening the night watches with what were then the stirring novelties of *Deus creator omnium* and *Aeterne rerum conditor*.[22]

It was a very different sort of crisis that almost nine hundred years later led to the writing of some of the other missal hymns, the great sacramental hymns of Saint Thomas Aquinas. It is a different sort of enemy that lies around the cathedral this time, but in some ways a more dangerous, for this one threatens not the doors of the cathedral but the very shrine of its innermost mystery, the Sacrament itself. The great age of scholasticism has reared its own triumphs, but the endless arguments of the time have had their hazards. For the more literal Latin mind was not always so instinctively at home with the mystical conceptions of the Greek world in which so much of the Christian faith had in the beginning defined itself, and the more matter-of-fact barbarian mind was even less so. At any rate the basic reality of the Sacrament of the Eucharist had been challenged, and Thomas Aquinas, so alert to the currents of thought of his day, so adroit in bringing even the modernities of his time into the defense of the Christian tradition, had addressed himself not so much to the defense as to the illumination of the truth in the great hymns of the Corpus Christi office.[23] A later age was to draw lines between the academic and the poetic as between the mystic and the scientific which, happily, Saint Thomas and his contemporaries at the court of Saint Louis never heard of. So the great Dominican carried his life-long battle to define an idea as clearly as possible into poetry, which has its own distinctive resources not always suspected by the more specialized logician. And the result is the great lyrics, *Lauda Sion Salvatorem* and *Pange Lingua*, which for nearly seven centuries now have won faith its warmest defender, love.

Or come to another age, close enough for us almost to touch, though a great chasm in some ways deeper than the six hundred years that separate King Louis and Queen Victoria has opened between us. The battle is now deep within the consciousness of man. Even for a man who has never lost his strong hold on the reality of God, there is the problem of conflicting traditions. So we find John Henry Newman in 1833, physically becalmed at sea in the strait between Corsica and Sardinia, and there in those long hours of weary thought forced to admit to himself the helplessness of one of the great religious minds of his time to tell where he is, to say nothing of where he should go.[24] Out of that spiritual becalming, a desperate thing for a man with his responsibilities not only for himself but for others, came the great surrender of the speculative casting himself upon the hidden providence of God and asking only for the light for the next step of the day's immediate necessity. So was born one of the great and most distinctive hymns of the modern world, "The Pillar of the Cloud:"

> Lead, Kindly Light, amid the encircling gloom
> Lead Thou me on!
> The night is dark, and I am far from home—
> Lead Thou me on!
> Keep Thou my feet; I do not ask to see
> The distant scene—one step enough for me.[25]

It is bracing for us today, beset not only with many uncertainties as man has always been, but with the shattering of illusions of irreversible progress and potential omnicompetence, to remember that out of the unending crises of Christian history have come some of the finest pledges, from the point of view of literature as well as religion, of the triumphant reality of Christian faith, very literally "out of the shadows light."

These crises have served to underscore a fact in man's spiritual history that has not always received its due regard, and that is the need for the perpetual renewal of the basic religious experience in terms of the context of each new age, indeed of each new life. The basis of our faith is an Incarnation, the penetration of the earthly by the Divine, of the temporal by the eternal. "Oh, Little Town of

Bethlehem" we shall be hearing very soon now, if the recent anticipation of the Christmas season on sidewalk and in store window has not already turned the record on. [This lecture was originally delivered early in December.] But the poets have always known with Saint Francis of Assisi, to whom the popularization if not the invention of the cribs we shall soon be dressing is usually ascribed,[26] that Bethlehem is really the village, great or small, in which we actually live here and now, the great task of all the Christmas poets is to bring that Babe into our inn. And so of every aspect of the life of Christ. What Saint Francis discovered in thirteenth-century Assisi, a drug-sodden wastrel rediscovered in nineteenth-century London. Francis Thompson is, of course, a minor figure beside the mighty masters of will and word whom I have cited above, but he has the heart of the matter in this challenge to his own doubting or indifferent contemporaries:

> The angels keep their ancient places;—
> Turn but a stone, and start a wing!
> 'Tis ye, 'tis your enstrangèd faces,
> That miss the many-splendoured thing.
>
> But (when so sad thou canst not sadder)
> Cry;—and upon thy so sore loss
> Shall shine the traffic of Jacob's ladder
> Pitched between Heaven and Charing Cross.[27]

Indeed, I am not sure but that in one respect Thompson's triumph may be greater than that of the original Francis. It was easier to conjure up the scenes of the New Testament in the relatively unspoiled Umbrian countryside than in the brick wildernesses of post-industrial London, with man's machines more and more insulating the children of the modern industrial world from the immemorial reminders of the natural creation, and we may add, all the more imperative for the preservation of man's very humanity.

The Thompson passage I have just read illustrates very well the great advantage to the Christian religious poet of the Incarnation. For the fact that his God became man and came into his world to share the pains and privileges of the terms of human existence opens up a whole range of poetic possibility. In the contemplation of Christ's earthly life the poet is freed of the anxieties of anthropomorphism and the fears of idolatry that have at various times stifled religious art. Particularly in ages of simple faith, untroubled by awareness of cultural pluralism or scruples of antiquarian accuracy, the opportunities opened are almost limitless. They range from the classic *Stabat mater dolorosa* of Jacopone da Todi,[28] with all its majestic passion and its power of statement, to the parochial homeliness of some of the anonymous lyrics of medieval England.

Indeed, the basic pattern of the whole genre is apparent in one of the oldest of these, a thoroughly primitive verse of the thirteenth century, and, it should be added, for that time a most uncharacteristically brief one:

> Nou goth sonne under wod,—
> me reweth, marie, thi faire Rode.
> Nou goth sonne under tre,—
> me reweth, marie, thi sone and the.[29]

This use of Our Lady as a bridge between the ordinary human being and her Son is, of course, one of the main humanizing devices of all this medieval lyric, as is most movingly apparent in the great Marian poems. In these the folk simplicity of the above can rise to great poetic distinction, as may be seen in what, I think, is the most perfect of all English Marian poems, a fifteenth-century lyric:

| I syng of a myden | that is makeles, |
| kyng of alle kynges | to here sone che ches. |

| he cam also stylle | ther his moder was |
| as dew in aprylle, | that fallyt on the gras. |

| he cam also stylle | to his moderes bowr |
| as dew in aprille, | that fallyt on the flour. |

| he can also stylle | ther his moder lay |
| as dew in aprille, | that fallyt on the spray. |

| moder and mayden | was never non but che— |
| wel may swych a lady | godes moder be.[30] |

There is, of course, nothing simple about the art of this poem in which so much is accomplished by suggestion and indirection. The very mystery of the Incarnation itself is used to suggest the perfect purity of the Virgin, with invocations of some of the most exquisite things in nature to invest the statement of that by now time-worn theme with all the freshness of the immemorial miracle of the coming of the spring.

This is, of course, a high point. But many of the loveliest of all medieval poems are Marian and when in English the reformers who feared the devotion to Mary won, the loss was great. Perhaps the most revealing testimony to the magnitude of that loss is a poem of the seventeenth-century Anglican, George Herbert, "To All Angels and Saints," in which the poet tells the Mother of God how gladly he would praise her but that he dares not from God's "garland steal, To make a posie for inferiour power."[31] In a queer, indirect fashion this wistful poem is one of the most telling tributes to the human need of Mary, and out of the camp of those who fear her, at that!

But though the basic human needs may change very little from age to age, the human emotions have their tides and seasons like everything else in the restless history of man. In one sense, it is all there in the psalms of David. But the awe of the classic can insulate as well as elevate. We need that fresh spark that is every so often struck off the hurrying wheels of Time's chariot to light the enduring ground of our human experience. That is where the poet, who is the voice of age to age succeeding, has his contribution to make.

Take, for example, one of the central themes of the long story of man's relation to God, the pull between God and the world. There is triumph in the opening of a brief

fourteenth-century poem that, like not a few
religious poems of that period, echoes some
of the conceits of the love poetry of the time:

> I hafe set my hert so hye,
> me likyt no love that lowere ys;
> And alle the paynes that y may drye,
> me thenk hyt do me good y-wis.[32]

But there is, also, the all too familiar tempor-
izing of human frailty in another poem of the
same century in which the key word *thole* may
be translated as "have patience":

> Louerd, thu clepedest me
> an ich nagt ne ansuarede the
> Bute wordes scloe and sclepie:
> 'thole yet! thole a litel!'
> Bute 'yiet' and 'yiet' was endelis,
> and 'thole a litel' a long wey is.[33]

By the seventeenth century the analysis of
consciousness has gone farther in poetry at

least, and so has the technique of the metaphysical poet for dealing with the complexity
of the resulting psychological patterns. George
Herbert might be cautious where the contemporary obsession on idolatry was concerned, but there was nothing timid in his
handling of his own personal problems, as may
be seen in his almost defiant ''The Collar''
with its dramatic and surprising end:

I struck the board, and cry'd, No more,
      I will abroad.
  What? shall I ever sigh and pine?
My lines and life are free; free as the rode,
  Loose as the winde, as large as store.
     Shall I be still in suit?
  Have I no harvest but a thorn
  To let me bloud, and not restore
What I have lost with cordiall fruit?
     Sure there was wine
Before my sighs did drie it: there was corn
  Before my tears did drown it.
Is the yeare onely lost to me?

Have I no bayes to crown it?
No flowers, no garlands gay? All blasted?
      All wasted?
  Not so, my heart: but there is fruit.
      And thou hast hands.
  Recover all thy sigh-blown age
On double pleasures: leave thy cold dispute
Of what is fit, and not. Forsake thy cage,
      Thy rope of sands,
Which pettie thoughts have made, and made to thee
  Good cable, to enforce and draw,
      And be thy law,
  While thou didst wink and wouldst not see.
      Away; take heed:
      I will abroad.
Call in thy deaths head there: tie up thy fears.
      He that forbears
  To suit and serve his need,
      Deserves his load.
But as I rav'd and grew more fierce and wilde
      At every word,
Me thoughts I heard one calling, *Childe!*
      And I reply'd, *My Lord.*[34]

The converse of Herbert's poem may be
seen in a twentieth-century poem in which

rather audaciously the old truancy of man is viewed from the divine point of view, and the divine regard for the individual is again given rather surprising expression, this time with that mixture of the homely and the sublime that is often found in contemporary Irish writers. It is James Stephens' ''What Tomas Said in a Pub'':

I saw God! Do you doubt it?
Do you dare to doubt it?
I saw the Almighty Man! His hand
Was resting on a mountain! And
He looked upon the World, and all about it:
I saw Him plainer than you see me now
—You mustn't doubt it!

He was not satisfied
His look was all dissatisfied!
His beard swung on a wind, far out of sight
Behind the world's curve! And there was light
Most fearful from His forehead! And he sighed
—That star went always wrong, and from the start
I was dissatisfied!—

He lifted up His hand!
I say He heaved a dreadful hand
Over the spinning earth! Then I said,—Stay,
You must not strike it, God! I'm in the way!
And I will never move from where I stand!—
He said,—Dear Child, I feared that you were dead,—
. . . And stayed His hand![35]

Though he would never, I am sure, have thought of looking for a vision of God in a pub, George Herbert would have appreciated the point of what this poet is trying to say. And so would the medieval poets whom I have already cited. For in this view of man's relation to his God, whatever one may say of its audacity, there is certainly none of that insulated Sabbath decorum that has so often threatened to wash all the color out of modern religious feeling.

From the fourth to the twentieth century, then, the poets have found an endless variety of ways of expressing man's awareness of his various relations to his God. And this variety extends to technique as well. In pictorical art and architecture we have been too often stultified with the notion that the style of the so-called ages of faith is forever to be imitated as peculiarly appropriate to the things of the faith, quite regardless of the fact that the twentieth century is a very different time with at least something approaching a style of its own, and still more of the fact that nothing was more characteristic of the medieval artist than his veritable passion for trying out at once the latest discovery in style or technique. The only thing that would have bothered a thirteenth-century artist about the twentieth-century experiment would have been how soon he could have brought it into the work already in hand. Not the medieval but the modern is the eternal idiom of the Christian, and the contemporary the appropriate occasion and context. So for poetry. The great emphasis on paradox and ambiguity in some of the current discussions of the new criticism has worried some traditionalists quite rightly because of a certain agnosticism that invests some of the particular discussions. But here, as so often, the problem is not in the techniques of the new poetry but in the purposes for which they are used. Paradox is an old tool of Christian thinking from the "happy fall" down. As an unknown fifteenth-century poet wrote rather jauntily in the Nativity song, "Adam lay I-bowndyn,":

Ne hadde the appil take ben, the appil take ben,
Ne hadde never our lady a ben hevene qwen;
Blyssid be the tyme that appil take was,
Ther-fore we mown syngyn, 'deo gracias!' [36]

And ambiguity in the sense of a tension between two certainties not easily resolved into a black-and-white *either/or* is the very habit of Christian thought, needless to say, a very different thing from a hovering between two uncertainties sometimes offered as the only version of ambiguity.

A very good example of the traditional use of paradox and ambiguity may be found in one of the most traditional poems of the great source and fountainhead of the modern metaphysical movement, John Donne himself. It is on the classic theme of the sinner's fear of the judgment of God—a thoroughly judicious, not to say justified; fear of Dr. Donne as of most of us.

A Hymne to God the Father

I

Wilt thou forgive that sinne where I begunne,
  Which was my sin, though it were done before?
Wilt thou forgive that sinne; through which I runne,
  And do run still: though still I do deplore?

When thou hast done, thou hast not done,
    For, I have more.

II

Wilt thou forgive that sinne which I have wonne
    Others to sinne? and, made my sinne their doore?
Wilt thou forgive that sinne which I did shunne
    A yeare, or two: but wallowed in, a score?
      When thou hast done, thou hast not done,
        For I have more.

III

I have a sinne of feare, that when I have spunne
    My last thred, I shall perish on the shore;
But sweare by thy selfe, that at my death thy sonne
    Shall shine as he shines now, and heretofore;
      And, having done that, Thou haste done,
        I feare no more.''[37]

Again, there will be those to whom a pun will seem unbecoming to repentance. Most Puritans of John Donne's day would have agreed with them. But like a genuine metaphysical, Donne would no more have thought of taking leave of his wit than of his wits just because he was sorry for his sins. Both wit and wits were the gift of God and to be sanctified by use in His service. But the issue of taste is a valid one. It is not just a matter of approval or disapproval, but of effectiveness for evoking the desired response. That effectiveness will vary with time, place, and person. If one does not like puns in religious lyrics or jokes in sermons, I do not see why he should not say so. He will find plenty of company, though not necessarily of the most cheerful. But he should be very careful about saying that other people should not enjoy puns, and especially should not have enjoyed them. Man's religious experience is a very spacious thing, and it would be a pity to set unnecessary bounds to the possibility of its expression, for there are odd balances in poetry as in all creative matters.

One of Donne's followers, Richard

Crashaw, admirably illustrates this. If I were asked to make a contribution to an anthology of religious horrors, I should be tempted to submit a couple of lines from his praise of "Sainte Mary Magdalene, or The Weeper," where he calls her weeping eyes:

> Two walking baths; two weeping motions;
> Portable, and compendious oceans.[38]

But if I were asked to contribute to an anthology of the sublimest verse in English literature, I should most certainly offer the invocation of the great Spanish mystic, Santa Teresa of Avila, that ends Crashaw's "The Flaming Heart":

> O thou undanted daughter of desires!
> By all thy dowr of LIGHTS and FIRES;
> By all the eagle in thee, all the dove;
> By all thy lives and deaths of love;
> By thy larg draughts of intellectuall day,
> And by thy thirsts of love more large then they;

By all thy brim-fill'd Bowles of feirce desire
By thy last Morning's draught of liquid fire;
By the full kingdome of that finall kisse
That seiz'd thy parting Soul, and seal'd thee his;
By all the heav'ns thou hast in him
Fair sister of the SERAPHIM!
By all of HIM we have in THEE;
Leave nothing of my SELF in me.
Let me so read thy life, that I
Unto all life of mine may dy.[39]

Ecstasy is a brittle business in poetry as in life. We are wise today to be chary of it when it can produce such atrocities as the description of the Magdalene's eyes, but it would be a pity if we laughed another Crashaw—if there could be another Crashaw—out of his progress from Mary Magdalene to Santa Teresa, and a tragedy if our more rationally disciplined imaginations lost their capacity to rise to the height of that praise of Santa Teresa. In religious poetry as in prayer the accent should be on the catholic, and that taken largely, for the ages as well as for the variety of man. "The world is charged with the grandeur of God," said the obscure Victorian poet who is the great precursor of the twentieth-century poetic style, Gerard Manley Hopkins. That simple sentence comes very close to summing up what the English religious lyrists have been saying from the thirteenth century to the twentieth. But in the second stanza of this little poem on "God's Grandeur" Hopkins takes our thoughts from the past to the inexhaustible future:

. . . nature is never spent;
  There lives the dearest freshness deep down things;
And though the last lights off the black West went
    Oh, morning, at the brown brink eastward,
      springs—
Because the Holy Ghost over the bent
    World broods with warm breast and with ah!
      bright wings.[40]

Prayer and Poetry

It is in this promise of the never-failing inspiration of the Holy Spirit that all our contemplations should end, in prayer and poetry alike.

Footnotes

1. Saint Augustine, *The Confessions* of, tr. E. B. Pusey, X, XXVII, 38.

2. S. T. Coleridge, *Biographia Literaria,* chap. 14.

3. Rom. vi:4.

4. Eph. iv:24.

5. Rudolph Otto, *Das Heilige* (München, 1936), pp. 6–7.

6. Exod. iii:5.

7. Luke xxiv:32.

8. *Aristotle on the Art of Fiction,* tr. L. J. Potts (Cambridge, 1953), chaps. 13–14.

9. Augustine, I, 1.

10. Luke ix:33.

11. Longinus, *On the Sublime,* tr. Benedict Einarson, 1945, sec. 7.

12. Matt. vii:7.

13. Augustine, I, V, 6.

14. T. S. Eliot, *After Strange Gods: A Primer of Modern Heresy* (New York, 1934), pp. 30–31.

15. Saint Bernard, *Life and Works* of, ed. Dom John Mabillon, tr. and ed. Samuel J. Eales (London, 1896), IV, 457ff.

16. Stéphane Mallarmé, *Poems,* tr. Roger Fry (New York, 1951), p. 91.

17. Matt. xxvii:46; Ps. xxi:2.

18. Angelus Walz, *Saint Thomas Aquinas* (Westminster, Md., 1951), pp. 97–98.

19. *Ibid;* Matthew Britt, ed., *The Hymns of the Breviary and Missal,* with preface by Hugh T. Henry (New York, 1922), pp. 126–8.

20. Augustine, IX, VII, 15.

21. F. Homes Dudden, *The Life and Times of St. Ambrose* (Oxford, 1935), I, 285–87.

22. *Ibid.*, I, 293–97.

23. Walz, pp. 97–99.

24. John Henry Newman, *Apologia Pro Vita Sua* (London, 1864), pp. 99–100.

25. John Henry Newman, *Selections from the Prose and Poetry* of, ed. Maurice Francis Egan (Cambridge, Mass., 1907), p. 289.

26. Omer Englebert, *Saint Francis of Assisi,* tr. and ed. Edward Hutton (London, 1950), pp. 270–71.

27. Francis Thompson, *Poems* of (New York, London, 1941), p. 293.

28. So ascribed by Britt, p. 134.

29. Carleton Brown, ed., *English Lyrics of the XIIIth Century* (Oxford, 1932), p. 1.

30. Carleton Brown, ed., *Religious Lyrics of the XVth Century* (Oxford, 1939), p. 119.

31. George Herbert, *The Works* of, ed. F. E. Hutchinson (Oxford, 1941), pp. 77–78.

32. Carleton Brown, ed., *Religious Lyrics of the XIVth Century*, rev. G. V. Smithers (Oxford, 1952), p. 229.

33. *Ibid.*, p. 3.

34. Herbert, pp. 153–54.

35. James Stephens, *Collected Poems* (New York, 1926) p. 131.

36. Brown, *Religious Lyrics of the XVth Century*, p. 120.

37. John Donne, *The Poems* of, ed. Herbert J. C. Grierson (Oxford, 1938), I, 369–70.

38. Richard Crashaw, *The Poems, English, Latin and Greek*, ed. L. C. Martin (Oxford, 1927), p. 312.

39. *Ibid.*, pp. 326–27.

40. Gerard Manley Hopkins, *Poems* of, ed. Robert Bridges; 2nd ed., Charles Williams (Oxford, 1935), p. 26.